Read & Play!

A dove is hiding on each page.
See if you can find them all!

This book is given with love:

_____

_____

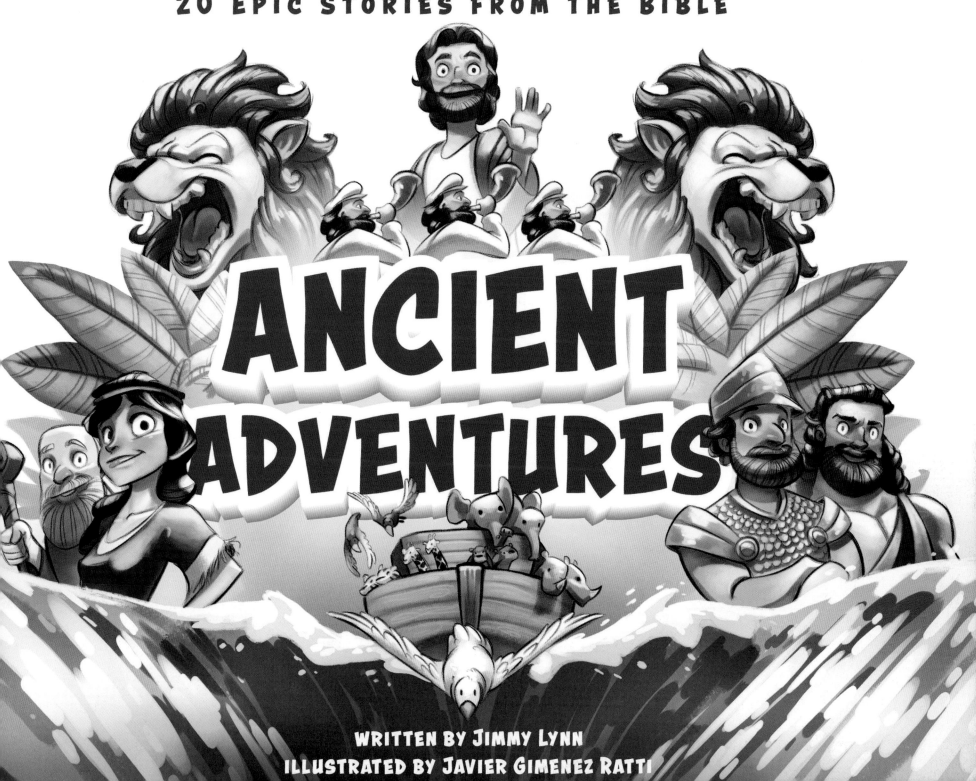

20 Epic Stories from the Bible

ANCIENT ADVENTURES

Written by Jimmy Lynn

Illustrated by Javier Gimenez Ratti

Creation

The most ancient of stories,
   before day or night,

God created the heavens...
   "Let there be light."

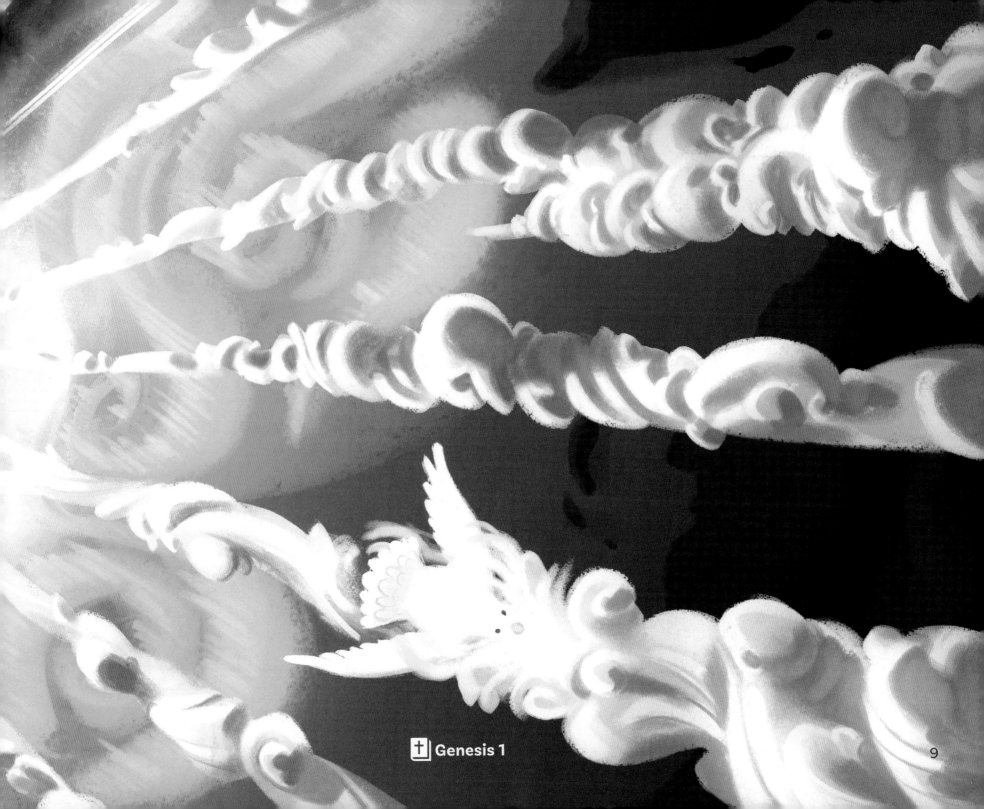

Adam & Eve

In His own image and likeness,
    God created the first man.

We all know him as Adam,
    the start of God's plan.

10

In a beautiful garden,
   where both Adam and Eve stood...

God had finished creation,
   and said, "It is good."

✝ Genesis 2-3

11

Noah

Noah built a great Ark,
  loading animals two by two...

40 days of rain and thunder,
  to start the world anew.

Abraham

As the father of a great nation,
   with children outnumbering the stars...

They became the people of Israel,
   a tribe very similar to ours.

Joseph

The blessed son of Jacob,
   his brothers sold him as a slave...

Rising up in Egypt,
   the entire nation he would save.

✝ Genesis 37–50

Moses

He parted the Red Sea,
   and pushed water to great heights...

Waves crashed down on the soldiers,
   freeing the Israelites.

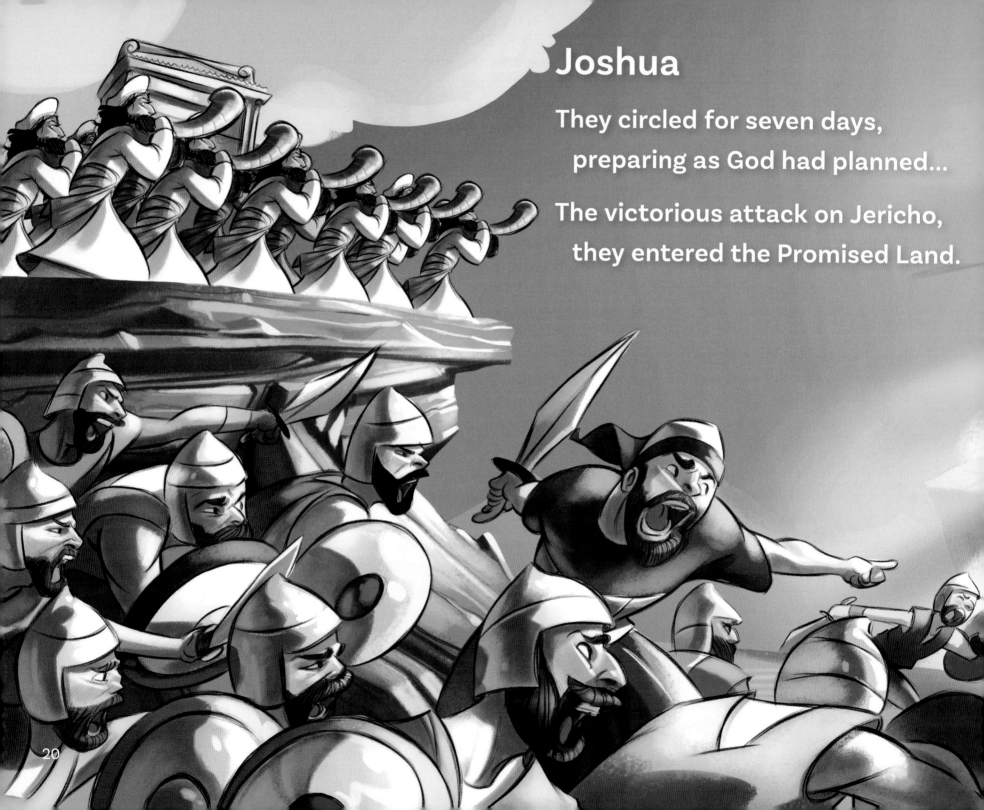

Joshua

They circled for seven days,
preparing as God had planned...

The victorious attack on Jericho,
they entered the Promised Land.

20

✝ **Numbers 13-14** and Joshua

21

✝ Judges 6-7

Gideon

A tiny army of 300,
   in cover of dark night...

A chaotic victory over Midian,
   fire, trumpets, and a fight.

Samson

Gaining strength from his long hair,
big muscles against the beast...

He shattered the temple's pillars,
crushing the Philistines at feast.

✝ Judges 13–16

David

A simple shepherd boy,
who would one day be a king...

His strength wasn't about size,
defeating Goliath with a sling.

1 Samuel 16-2 Samuel

Elijah

A true prophet of God,

he was blessed with divine forces...

Racing off to the heavens...

in a chariot of flaming, fire horses.

Jonah

Running away from God,
  swallowed by a fish with a spout…

He promised to deliver God's message,
  so the whale spit him out.

Jonah

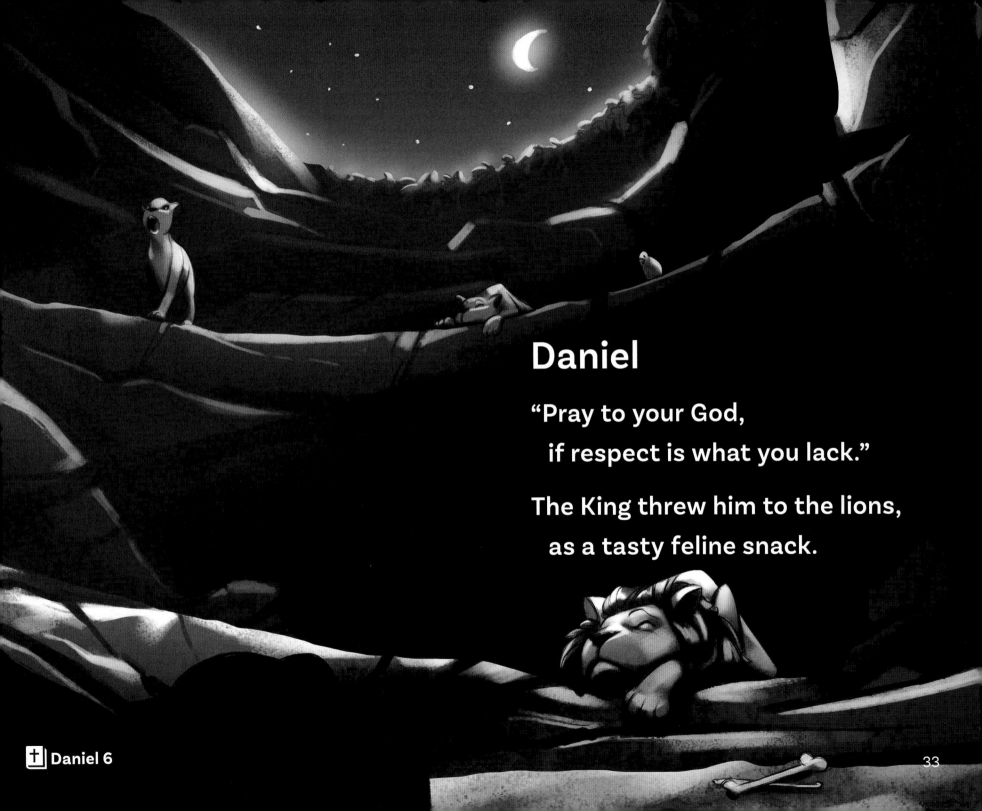

Daniel

"Pray to your God,
if respect is what you lack."

The King threw him to the lions,
as a tasty feline snack.

Esther

From India to Ethiopia,
  in cities big and small...

The Queen had saved her people,
  the King would spare them all.

34   ✝ Esther

Three Wise-Men

Three wise men approached,
  with gifts for the new King...

Guided by a bright star,
  hope for us He would bring.

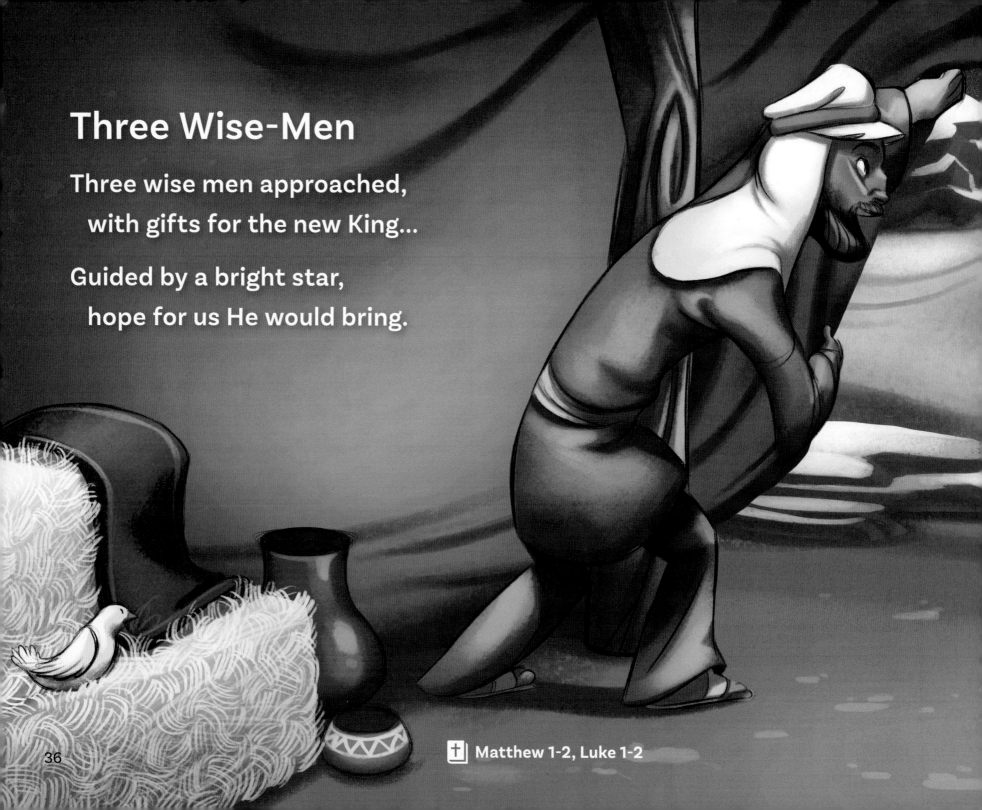

Matthew 1-2, Luke 1-2

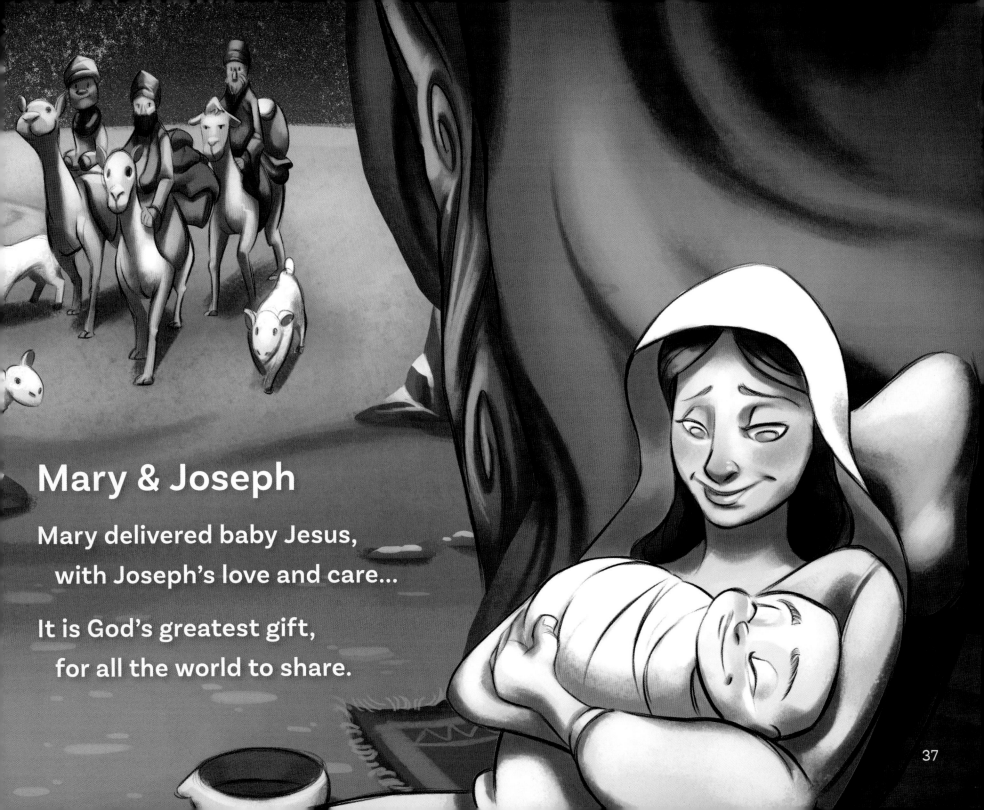

Mary & Joseph

Mary delivered baby Jesus,
  with Joseph's love and care...

It is God's greatest gift,
  for all the world to share.

37

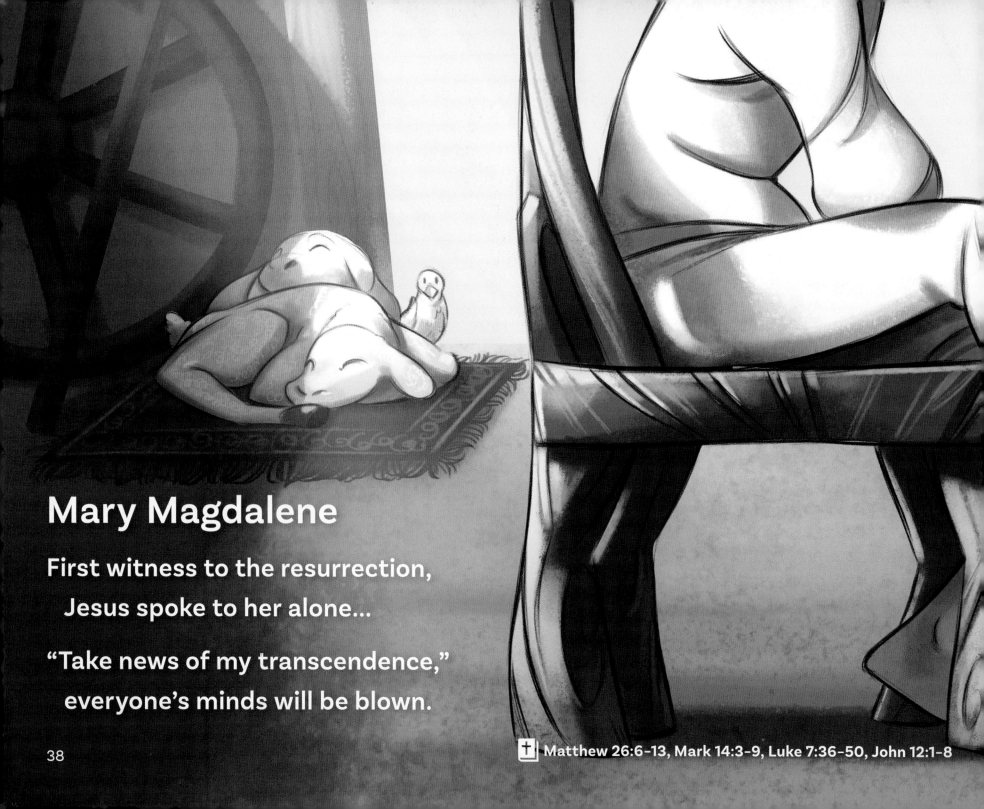

Mary Magdalene

First witness to the resurrection,
Jesus spoke to her alone...

"Take news of my transcendence,"
everyone's minds will be blown.

✝ Matthew 26:6–13, Mark 14:3–9, Luke 7:36–50, John 12:1–8

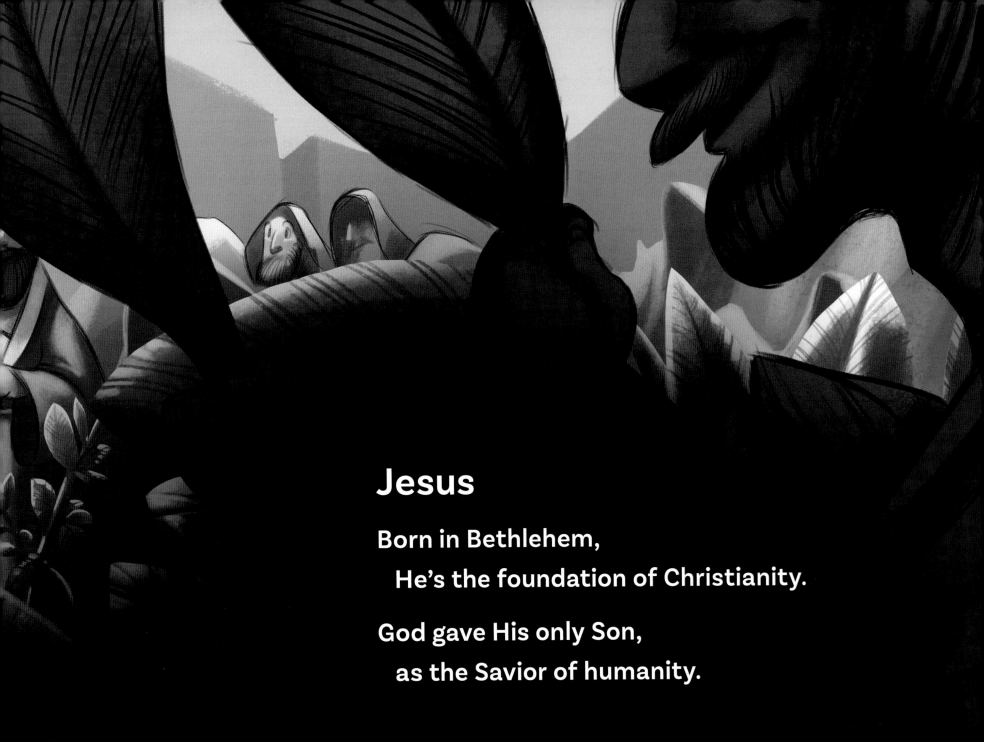

Jesus

Born in Bethlehem,
  He's the foundation of Christianity.

God gave His only Son,
  as the Savior of humanity.

✝ Matthew, Mark, Luke, and John

As your evening winds down,
and you turn off the bedroom light...

There will be more of His stories tomorrow,
say a prayer and then good night.

43

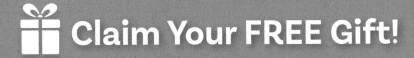 **Claim Your FREE Gift!**

Visit ➡ PDICBooks.com/ancient

Thank you for purchasing Ancient Adventures,
and welcome to the Puppy Dogs & Ice Cream family.

We're certain you're going to love the little gift
we've prepared for you at the website above.